FORMENTERA

Travel guide 2025

Discover the Best Places, Local Experiences, and Practical Tips for a Memorable Trip

Gideon Riven

Copyright © 2024 by Gideon Riven

Table of Contents

Welcome to Formentera

An Overview

Formentera, the smallest of Spain's Balearic Islands, is a true Mediterranean gem known for its untouched beaches, crystal-clear waters, and laid-back island vibe. Located just south of Ibiza, Formentera offers a more relaxed and tranquil atmosphere compared to its neighboring island's vibrant party scene. Often called the "last paradise of the Mediterranean," this serene destination is perfect for travelers seeking a peaceful escape, where they can unwind, enjoy nature, and explore the island's hidden treasures.

This compact island, just 83 square kilometers, is easy to explore, with unspoiled beaches and scenic countryside that's ideal for cycling, hiking, and water activities. Whether you're lounging on white sandy shores, diving in the pristine waters, or visiting ancient lighthouses, Formentera feels like a world away from the hustle and bustle of the mainland. With its small population and commitment to sustainable tourism, Formentera offers a rare chance to experience the Mediterranean at its most authentic.

Why Visit Formentera?

Formentera is a destination for those who value simplicity, natural beauty, and a slower pace of life. Unlike the larger Balearic Islands, Formentera has managed to preserve its rustic charm and pristine environment, making it a paradise for nature lovers. Its famous turquoise waters and white-sand beaches are among the best in Europe, offering a perfect backdrop for swimming, snorkeling, and sunbathing.

Formentera also attracts visitors interested in eco-tourism, thanks to its sustainable travel practices, local organic farms, and efforts to preserve its natural resources. The island's modest size makes it easy to explore on foot, by bicycle, or scooter, making it a haven for outdoor enthusiasts. Whether you are looking to enjoy a peaceful retreat or indulge in water sports like windsurfing and sailing, Formentera has something for everyone.

A visit to Formentera promises an authentic island experience with friendly locals, traditional Spanish cuisine, and stunning landscapes that will leave a lasting impression. The island's commitment to responsible tourism ensures that future generations will continue to enjoy this Mediterranean paradise in its purest form.

Highlights for Travelers

Ses Illetes Beach: Often ranked as one of the best beaches in the world, Ses Illetes boasts powdery white sand and shallow, crystal-clear waters. It's perfect for sunbathing, swimming, or renting a boat for the day.

Cala Saona: This small bay is known for its vivid sunsets, making it a popular spot for evening relaxation. With its calm waters, it's great for swimming and snorkeling.

La Mola Lighthouse: Perched on the island's highest point, this iconic lighthouse offers panoramic views over the Mediterranean. It's an excellent spot for photography and soaking in the island's rugged beauty.

Sant Francesc Xavier: The island's charming capital is filled with whitewashed buildings, cozy cafes, and boutique shops. It's the perfect place to explore local life and enjoy a relaxed meal.

Ses Salines Natural Park: A protected area of salt flats, dunes, and wetlands, this park is home to diverse wildlife, including flamingos. It's a peaceful spot for a nature walk.

Cycling Routes: With its flat terrain and scenic routes, Formentera is a cyclist's paradise. Renting a bike is one of the best ways to explore the island's hidden corners.

Quick Facts About Formentera

Location: Southernmost island of the Balearic Islands, Spain.

Size: Approximately 83 square kilometers (32 square miles).

Population: Around 12,000 residents.

Language: Catalan and Spanish are the official languages.

Currency: Euro (€).

Time Zone: Central European Time (CET) in winter, Central European Summer Time (CEST) in summer.

Climate: Mediterranean climate with hot, dry summers and mild winters. Ideal beach weather from May to September.

Best Time to Visit: Late spring to early autumn (May–October) for beach lovers. The off-season is perfect for those seeking solitude.

Top Travel Tips for First-Time Visitors

Ferry Travel from Ibiza: The only way to reach Formentera is by ferry from Ibiza. Ferries run frequently, but it's advisable to book tickets in advance, especially in peak season.

Rent a Scooter or Bike: Formentera's compact size and scenic paths make it ideal for exploring on two wheels. Renting a scooter or bicycle gives you the freedom to visit remote beaches and hidden coves at your own pace.

Bring Cash: While most places accept credit cards, some smaller shops and restaurants prefer cash, especially in rural areas.

Sunscreen and Water: The Mediterranean sun can be intense, so pack plenty of high-SPF sunscreen and stay hydrated throughout the day.

Nude Beaches: Many beaches on Formentera are unofficially nudist-friendly, particularly the more secluded ones. Be prepared for a relaxed attitude towards nudity.

Respect Nature: Formentera's natural environment is protected, so be mindful of littering and avoid disturbing the wildlife. Many beaches are part of protected reserves, so follow local guidelines to help preserve these beautiful ecosystems.

Book Accommodation Early: Formentera is a popular summer destination, and accommodation can fill up quickly. It's best to book your stay well in advance if you're visiting between June and September.

Visit Off-Peak for Tranquility: If you want to avoid crowds, plan your visit in May or September. The weather is still warm, but the island is quieter, and prices for accommodation and rentals are lower.

Island Etiquette: Formentera maintains a relaxed and respectful atmosphere. Dress modestly in towns and always greet locals with a friendly "Hola" or "Bon dia" (in Catalan).

Stay Eco-Friendly: Formentera promotes sustainable tourism, so make efforts to reduce waste, recycle, and use eco-friendly products during your stay.

Chapter 1

Planning Your Trip

Planning a trip to Formentera involves a mix of practical considerations and excitement as you prepare for a journey to one of the Mediterranean's most tranquil islands. Known for its pristine beaches, clear waters, and relaxed atmosphere, Formentera offers a unique escape from the hustle and bustle of everyday life. In this chapter, we will cover everything you need to know to ensure a smooth and enjoyable trip, including the best time to visit, how to get to the island, budgeting tips, and important health and safety guidelines.

Best Time to Visit Formentera

Formentera is a year-round destination, but the best time to visit largely depends on what kind of experience you're looking for.

Summer (June to September): This is the peak tourist season when the island is at its most vibrant. The weather is hot, with temperatures ranging from 25°C to 30°C (77°F to 86°F), making it ideal for beach activities, swimming, and water sports. However, this is also when the island is busiest, so you can expect higher prices for accommodations and services. If you love the buzz of summer crowds, lively beach bars, and long sunny days, this is the perfect time to visit.

Spring (April to June): For those who prefer milder weather and fewer crowds, late spring is an excellent choice. Temperatures range from 18°C to 24°C (64°F to 75°F), making it comfortable for outdoor activities like cycling, hiking, and sightseeing. The island is lush with blooming flowers, and you'll still have plenty of warm days for beach outings. This period is also less expensive compared to peak summer months.

Autumn (September to October): Early autumn, particularly September, offers similar benefits to spring. The weather is still warm, and the sea temperature remains pleasant for swimming. Prices begin to drop as the tourist season winds down, but the island retains its relaxed charm. This is an ideal time for couples, solo travelers, or those looking for a quieter escape.

Winter (November to March): Winter in Formentera is mild, with temperatures averaging between 10°C and 15°C (50°F to 59°F). While it's too cool for swimming, this is the time to visit if you're seeking solitude and peaceful walks along deserted beaches. Many tourist facilities, including hotels and restaurants, may close for the season, so it's essential to plan ahead if you're visiting during this time.

Weather by Season: When to Go

The weather in Formentera is typically Mediterranean, characterized by hot, dry summers and mild winters. Below is a breakdown of the weather you can expect during each season:

Spring (April to June): Average daytime temperatures range from 18°C to 24°C (64°F to 75°F). Rain is minimal, and the days grow longer, making it perfect for exploring the island on foot or by bike.

Summer (June to September): Temperatures soar to 25°C–30°C (77°F–86°F) with very little rain. The sun shines for an average of 11 hours a day, offering ideal beach weather.

Autumn (September to November): September remains warm with temperatures around 24°C (75°F), but by November, they drop to about 15°C (59°F). Rain becomes more frequent, particularly in October and November.

Winter (December to March): Daytime temperatures in winter are mild, between 10°C and 15°C (50°F–59°F). It's cooler at night, and there's more rainfall compared to other seasons.

How to Get to Formentera

Formentera does not have an airport, so the only way to reach the island is by ferry. Most travelers arrive via Ibiza, as the ferry connection between the two islands is frequent and efficient. However, it's also possible to catch ferries from mainland Spain, though this is less common.

Ferries from Ibiza and Mainland Spain

The main gateway to Formentera is the nearby island of Ibiza, which has an international airport serving flights from major European cities. From Ibiza, regular ferries operate between Ibiza Town (Eivissa) and Formentera, with journey times ranging from 30 to 60 minutes, depending on the service.

Ferries from Ibiza: Several companies, including Balearia, Trasmapi, and Mediterranea Pitiusa, operate ferries between Ibiza Town and La Savina, Formentera's main port. The ferries run multiple times daily, especially during the summer season. High-speed services can get you to Formentera in as little as 30 minutes, while standard ferries take around 50–60 minutes. Prices vary based on the season, with return tickets typically costing between €40 and €60 per person during peak times.

Ferries from Mainland Spain: You can also travel to Formentera by ferry from mainland Spanish cities such as Barcelona, Valencia, or Denia. These ferries dock in Ibiza, where you'll need to transfer to a ferry bound for Formentera. The overall journey is longer, but it can be a scenic and enjoyable way to travel.

Travel Routes and Connections

If you're flying from an international destination, you will first need to book a flight to Ibiza. Ibiza's airport (Aeropuerto de Ibiza) has direct flights from many European cities, especially during the summer months. From the airport, you can take a taxi or bus to Ibiza Town's ferry port, which is approximately 15 minutes away. Once at the ferry terminal, you can purchase tickets for the next available boat to Formentera.

To avoid waiting in line during peak season, it's advisable to book your ferry tickets online in advance. Most ferry companies offer flexible tickets, so you can change your departure time if needed.

Entry Requirements and Visas

Formentera is part of Spain, which is a member of the European Union (EU) and the Schengen Area.

EU/EEA Citizens: Travelers from the EU or EEA countries can enter Formentera with a valid national ID card or passport. No visa is required for stays of up to 90 days.

Non-EU Citizens: Citizens of countries outside the EU may require a Schengen visa to enter Spain. Check with your local Spanish embassy or consulate to confirm the visa requirements for your nationality. If you are a citizen of a country that enjoys visa-free travel to the Schengen Area, you can stay in Formentera for up to 90 days within a 180-day period without a visa.

Ensure your passport is valid for at least three months beyond your planned departure date from the Schengen Area.

Budgeting for Formentera

Formentera can be a relatively expensive destination, especially during the peak summer months. However, with careful planning, you can tailor your trip to suit different budgets, whether you're looking for a luxury experience or a more affordable getaway.

Cost Breakdown: Luxury, Mid-Range, Budget

Luxury: If you're seeking a luxurious stay, you'll find plenty of high-end accommodation options, including boutique hotels, private villas, and beachfront resorts. Expect to spend upwards of €300 per night on accommodation, with gourmet dining experiences costing €100+ per meal. Private boat charters, spa treatments, and exclusive beach clubs can add to your overall costs.

Mid-Range: Mid-range travelers can enjoy comfortable accommodation in guesthouses, boutique hotels, or well-rated apartments, with prices ranging from €100 to €250 per night. Meals at casual restaurants and tapas bars cost between €15 and €40 per person. Renting a scooter or bicycle is a popular and affordable way to explore the island, costing around €10–€30 per day.

Budget: For budget-conscious travelers, staying in hostels, budget guesthouses, or camping can help keep costs down, with accommodation ranging from €40 to €100 per night. Many affordable dining options, such as beachside snack bars and takeaways, offer meals for under €15. Self-catering is also a cost-effective option, with local supermarkets selling fresh produce, bread, and seafood.

Currency, ATMs, and Tipping Culture

Formentera uses the euro (€), and you'll find ATMs throughout the main towns, including La Savina, Es Pujols, and Sant Francesc Xavier. Credit cards are widely accepted in most restaurants, shops, and hotels, but it's advisable to carry some cash, especially when visiting rural areas or beachside cafes where card payments may not be possible.

Tipping: Tipping is appreciated but not obligatory in Spain. In restaurants, a tip of 5% to 10% is considered generous if you've received good service. It's also customary to leave a small tip for hotel staff and taxi drivers.

Health and Safety Guidelines

Formentera is generally a safe destination with low crime rates, but it's always wise to take precautions to ensure a safe and healthy trip.

Sun Protection: The Mediterranean sun can be strong, especially in the summer. Pack high-SPF sunscreen, a wide-brimmed hat, and sunglasses to protect yourself from sunburn. Stay hydrated by drinking plenty of water throughout the day.

Mosquitoes: In the warmer months, mosquitoes can be a nuisance, especially near wetlands and rural areas. Bring insect repellent and wear long sleeves in the evening to avoid bites.

Swimming Safety: While Formentera's beaches are generally safe for swimming, it's important to respect local guidelines. Pay attention to the colored flags on beaches that indicate swimming conditions—red means dangerous, yellow means caution, and green means it's safe to swim.

Emergency Numbers: In case of an emergency, dial 112 for assistance. This number works for police, ambulance, and fire services throughout Spain.

Travel Insurance and Emergency Contacts

Travel insurance is highly recommended when visiting Formentera. Ensure that your policy covers medical emergencies, trip cancellations, lost luggage, and any activities you plan to undertake, such as water sports. European travelers with a European Health Insurance Card (EHIC) are entitled to state-provided healthcare in Spain, but travel insurance is still advisable to cover private healthcare costs or repatriation.

Keep a list of emergency contacts, including your travel insurance provider's helpline and local medical facilities. For medical assistance on the island, the **Formentera Hospital** in Sant Francesc Xavier is the main healthcare facility.

Sustainable Travel: How to Visit Formentera Responsibly

Formentera is committed to sustainable tourism, with initiatives in place to protect its fragile environment. As a visitor, you can contribute to the island's preservation by adopting eco-friendly habits:

Use Public Transport or Rent a Bike: The island's small size makes it perfect for exploring by bike or on foot. By reducing car usage, you help minimize pollution and congestion. If you need to rent a vehicle, consider an electric scooter or car.

Respect Nature Reserves: Formentera's beaches and nature reserves, like Ses Salines Natural Park, are protected areas.

Follow local guidelines, such as staying on designated paths, avoiding littering, and not disturbing wildlife.

Choose Eco-Friendly Accommodations: Many hotels and guesthouses on the island follow sustainable practices, such as water conservation and waste reduction. Support these businesses to encourage environmentally friendly tourism.

Reduce Plastic Waste: Bring a reusable water bottle, and avoid using single-use plastics during your stay. Many establishments offer water refill stations, and the tap water in Formentera is safe to drink.

Chapter 2

Luxury Accommodations

Gecko Hotel & Beach Club

Features: A beachfront hotel offering an exclusive experience with an infinity pool, private beach access, spa treatments, and yoga classes. Rooms are modern and spacious, with sea views and private terraces.

Offers: Full-service spa, beachfront dining, wellness programs, and outdoor fitness activities.

Price: Estimated at €400 to €700 per night depending on the season.

Proximity: Located on Playa Migjorn, it's within walking distance of the beach and close to local restaurants and bars. The capital, Sant Francesc, is a 10-minute drive away.

Suitability: Ideal for couples, honeymooners, and solo travelers seeking luxury and relaxation.

Website: geckobeachclub.com

Can Tres Formentera

Features: This boutique property offers luxurious self-catering apartments and villas, each with modern interiors and private gardens or terraces.

Offers: Apartments with full kitchens, a communal outdoor pool, and free bike rentals.

Price: Around €350 to €600 per night.

Proximity: Located near Playa Migjorn, it's a short drive from Es Caló and La Mola Lighthouse.

Suitability: Great for families or groups of friends, but also suitable for solo travelers seeking privacy.

Website: cantresformentera.com

Hotel Es Marès

Features: A stylish hotel offering a combination of modern amenities and traditional Formentera architecture. The hotel features a spa, gourmet restaurant, and a serene courtyard.

Offers: Spa services, fine dining, and complimentary breakfast.

Price: Between €300 and €500 per night.

Proximity: Located in the heart of Sant Francesc Xavier, it's within walking distance of shops, cafes, and historical sites.

Suitability: Perfect for solo travelers or couples who want to explore Formentera's cultural side.

Website: hotelesmares.com

Five Flowers Hotel & Spa Formentera

Features: A 5-star property offering a rooftop pool, panoramic sea views, and a luxurious spa. Rooms come with modern amenities and private balconies.

Offers: Rooftop dining, wellness center, and complimentary shuttle service to nearby beaches.

Price: Ranges from €450 to €750 per night.

Proximity: Located in Es Pujols, it's near nightlife, restaurants, and the popular Ses Illetes Beach.

Suitability: Best suited for luxury travelers, including solo visitors looking for a high-end experience.

Website: fiveflowershotel.com

Casa Pacha Formentera

Features: Part of the iconic Pacha group, this beachfront hotel offers high-end service with minimalist design, sea views, and an exclusive beachfront restaurant.

Offers: Direct beach access, wellness services, and curated experiences.

Price: Approximately €500 to €800 per night.

Proximity: Located on Migjorn Beach, it's perfect for those looking to relax by the water while still being a short drive to Sant Francesc.

Suitability: Ideal for couples and solo travelers seeking a tranquil, upscale retreat.

Website: pachahotelformentera.com

Mid-Range Accommodations

Apartamentos Castaví

Features: Fully equipped modern apartments with kitchenettes, private balconies, and a communal pool. The apartments are clean, spacious, and offer a relaxed stay.

Offers: Pool, free Wi-Fi, kitchen facilities, and an on-site restaurant.

Price: €150 to €250 per night.

Proximity: Located in Es Pujols, it's a short walk to the beach and near local nightlife.

Suitability: Great for solo travelers, families, and groups looking for flexibility in their stay.

Website: apartamentoscastavi.com

Hotel Cala Saona & Spa

Features: A beachfront hotel with contemporary rooms offering sea views, a large pool, and a full-service spa. The hotel also has direct beach access.

Offers: Spa services, outdoor pool, and beachfront dining.

Price: Ranges from €180 to €300 per night.

Proximity: Located on Cala Saona Beach, it's ideal for those who want direct access to the sea and sunsets.

Suitability: Suitable for couples and solo travelers looking for a mid-range beachside escape.

Website: hotelcalasaona.com

Es Pi 2 Hotel

Features: A simple, cozy hotel offering traditional-style rooms with basic amenities. It has a peaceful atmosphere and provides breakfast.

Offers: Complimentary breakfast, Wi-Fi, and free parking.

Price: Around €120 to €200 per night.

Proximity: Close to Playa Migjorn, a quiet area yet within easy reach of local bars and restaurants.

Suitability: Ideal for solo travelers and couples who want a budget-friendly, comfortable stay.

Website: espi2hotel.com

Hotel Blanco Formentera

Features: A modern hotel with chic decor, outdoor pool, and a rooftop terrace. Rooms are sleek and come with modern amenities.

Offers: Rooftop bar, pool, and complimentary breakfast.

Price: Estimated at €180 to €300 per night.

Proximity: Located in Es Pujols, it's close to restaurants, bars, and the beach.

Suitability: Perfect for solo travelers and couples who want a balance of comfort and style at a reasonable price.

Website: hotelblancoformentera.com

Insotel Club Formentera Playa

Features: A beachfront resort with various room types, including suites and apartments, offering direct beach access, several swimming pools, and a variety of dining options.

Offers: All-inclusive options, sports facilities, and organized activities.

Price: €160 to €280 per night.

Proximity: Situated on Playa Migjorn, it's close to popular beaches and a short drive to Sant Francesc.

Suitability: Ideal for families and solo travelers who want an all-inclusive experience at a mid-range price.

Website: insotelhotelgroup.com

Budget Accommodations

Hostal Rafalet

Features: A budget-friendly hostal with basic, clean rooms and a traditional restaurant. Many rooms have balconies overlooking the sea.

Offers: Restaurant, free Wi-Fi, and a relaxed atmosphere.

Price: €70 to €100 per night.

Proximity: Located in Es Caló, it's close to the beach and local shops.

Suitability: Great for solo travelers on a budget looking for a peaceful, affordable stay.

Website: hostalrafalet.com

Hostal Bellavista

Features: Simple, no-frills rooms with basic amenities and a small on-site restaurant. The hostal offers good value for those seeking a low-cost option.

Offers: Restaurant, free Wi-Fi, and basic breakfast.

Price: €60 to €90 per night.

Proximity: Located in La Savina, it's near the ferry port and within walking distance of the marina.

Suitability: Suitable for solo travelers and backpackers looking for a budget option with easy access to transportation.

Website: hostalbellavista.com

Camping La Playa

Features: A camping site offering affordable pitches for tents, caravans, and basic bungalows. It's a great way to experience Formentera's natural environment.

Offers: On-site restaurant, bike rentals, and shared bathroom facilities.

Price: €40 to €80 per night for a tent pitch or bungalow.

Proximity: Located near Playa Migjorn, it's within walking distance of the beach.

Suitability: Ideal for solo travelers and adventure seekers looking for a budget-friendly outdoor experience.

Website: campinglaplaya.com

Hostal Alemania

Features: A small, family-run guesthouse with basic rooms and a friendly atmosphere. Rooms are simple but well-kept, and some offer views of the sea.

Offers: Free Wi-Fi and complimentary breakfast.

Price: €70 to €90 per night.

Proximity: Located in Es Pujols, close to restaurants, bars, and the beach.

Suitability: Suitable for solo travelers looking for affordable accommodation in a central location.

Website: hostalalemania.com

Hostal Bon Sol

Features: A budget-friendly guesthouse with bright, functional rooms. It's a no-frills accommodation, but offers excellent value for money.

Offers: Free Wi-Fi and basic breakfast.

Price: €50 to €80 per night.

Proximity: Situated in Sant Ferran, it's a short walk from local bars, restaurants, and a few kilometers from the beach.

Suitability: Perfect for solo travelers and backpackers seeking a clean, budget-friendly place to stay.

Website: hostalbonsol.com

Chapter 3

Top Attractions and Must-See Sights

Formentera may be small, but it's packed with natural beauty, history, and cultural treasures. From pristine beaches and scenic lighthouses to charming towns and historical landmarks, this chapter covers the island's top attractions and must-see sights, giving you a well-rounded experience of this Mediterranean gem.

Ses Illetes Beach: The Crown Jewel of Formentera

Often regarded as one of the best beaches in Europe, **Ses Illetes Beach** is the crown jewel of Formentera. Located on the island's northern tip, within the Ses Salines Natural Park, it boasts powdery white sands and shallow, crystal-clear turquoise waters, making it perfect for swimming and sunbathing. Its tranquil beauty draws visitors from all over the world, but despite its popularity, it has retained a peaceful atmosphere.

What to Do: Spend the day relaxing on the soft sand, swim in the calm waters, or take a boat tour around the nearby islets. Windsurfing and paddleboarding are also popular here due to the shallow waters.

Best Time to Visit: Early morning or late afternoon to avoid the peak crowds.

Suitability: Ideal for couples, families, and solo travelers who want to experience a world-class beach.

Proximity: It's about 5 kilometers from La Savina port, easily reachable by bike, car, or bus.

Notes: This beach is part of a protected nature reserve, so expect to pay a small fee for parking and access in peak season.

Cala Saona: Formentera's Best Sunset Spot

Cala Saona is a small, secluded bay on the island's west coast, known for its stunning sunset views. With its calm, shallow waters surrounded by reddish cliffs, Cala Saona is perfect for a laid-back beach day, offering a more intimate and relaxed setting compared to other busier beaches.

What to Do: Enjoy swimming and snorkeling in the clear water, or simply relax on the beach as you wait for the spectacular sunset. For those who enjoy hiking, there are nearby trails that offer panoramic views of the coastline.

Best Time to Visit: Late afternoon to enjoy the sunset.

Suitability: Perfect for couples and solo travelers seeking a quieter beach experience. Families will also find it suitable thanks to the calm waters.

Proximity: About 8 kilometers from Sant Francesc Xavier, accessible by car, bike, or scooter.

Notes: There are a few small beach bars where you can grab drinks and snacks, but it's worth bringing your own refreshments for a full day at the beach.

La Mola Lighthouse: Scenic Views and History

The **La Mola Lighthouse** (Faro de La Mola) is one of Formentera's most iconic landmarks, located on the island's easternmost point. Perched on dramatic cliffs, it offers sweeping views over the Mediterranean Sea and is often described as the "end of the world." The lighthouse, built in 1861, also holds historical significance as a navigational aid for sailors and is an inspiration for artists and writers, including Jules Verne.

What to Do: Visit the lighthouse for its breathtaking views and learn about its history at the small exhibit inside. The surrounding cliffs are also a fantastic spot for photography or a peaceful walk.

Best Time to Visit: Early morning or late afternoon for the best lighting and fewer visitors.

Suitability: Ideal for solo travelers, couples, and photographers who enjoy scenic landscapes and history.

Proximity: Located near El Pilar de la Mola, about 15 kilometers from Sant Francesc Xavier.

Notes: There is a local market in the nearby village of La Mola on Wednesdays and Sundays, where you can buy handmade crafts and souvenirs.

Ses Salines Natural Park: A Protected Paradise

Ses Salines Natural Park spans across the northern tip of Formentera and the southern part of Ibiza. This UNESCO World Heritage site is known for its diverse ecosystems, including salt flats, wetlands, sand dunes, and beaches. The park is a haven for birdwatchers, with species like flamingos frequenting the area, and it also features some of Formentera's most stunning beaches.

What to Do: Explore the salt flats, which turn pink at certain times of the year, take a nature walk through the wetlands, or visit the beaches within the park for swimming and relaxation.

Best Time to Visit: Early morning or late afternoon for a peaceful experience and cooler temperatures.

Suitability: Perfect for nature lovers, birdwatchers, and families interested in eco-friendly activities.

Proximity: The park covers a large area, but its entrance is easily accessible from La Savina or Es Pujols.

Notes: Be sure to bring water and sun protection, as there is little shade along the walking paths.

Es Pujols: The Lively Resort Town

Es Pujols is Formentera's main resort town, known for its vibrant atmosphere, beachfront restaurants, bars, and lively nightlife. It's a great base for travelers who want a mix of beach relaxation and evening entertainment. The beach at Es Pujols is well-maintained, with soft sand and clear water, making it a popular spot for both tourists and locals.

What to Do: Spend the day on the beach, dine at one of the many beachfront restaurants, or explore the town's shops. In the evening, the nightlife comes alive with bars, lounges, and clubs catering to a range of tastes.

Best Time to Visit: Daytime for the beach, or after sunset for nightlife.

Suitability: Ideal for solo travelers, groups of friends, and couples looking for a lively, central location.

Proximity: Located on the northern coast, Es Pujols is about 5 kilometers from La Savina and easily reachable by bike, car, or bus.

Notes: It's the most developed area of the island, so expect more crowds and higher prices compared to other parts of Formentera.

Sant Francesc Xavier: Formentera's Charming Capital

The island's capital, **Sant Francesc Xavier**, is a charming and quiet town where traditional whitewashed buildings line narrow streets. It's the cultural heart of Formentera, offering a slower pace compared to the bustling coastal areas. The town square is home to the island's main church, the 18th-century **Església de Sant Francesc Xavier**, as well as local cafes, boutiques, and markets.

What to Do: Visit the church, explore the local shops and cafes, and relax in the town square. The town is a great place to pick up souvenirs, including local crafts and artwork.

Best Time to Visit: Late morning or early afternoon when the shops and cafes are open.

Suitability: Ideal for solo travelers and couples who want to experience Formentera's local life and culture.

Proximity: Located inland, Sant Francesc is about 3 kilometers from La Savina.

Notes: The town is small, so it's easy to explore on foot in just a few hours.

Historical Landmarks and Cultural Sights

Formentera is not just about beaches; the island has a rich history that's reflected in its landmarks and cultural sites. A visit to these places will give you a deeper understanding of Formentera's heritage and the people who have lived there throughout the centuries.

The Ethnological Museum of Formentera

The **Ethnological Museum** is located in Sant Francesc Xavier and is dedicated to preserving and showcasing the island's history and traditional way of life. It displays various artifacts, including agricultural tools, traditional clothing, and household items used by the island's residents in past centuries.

What to Do: Explore the museum's exhibits to learn about the island's agricultural and fishing traditions, as well as its architecture and folklore.

Best Time to Visit: Anytime during opening hours, but check for seasonal schedules.

Suitability: Great for history enthusiasts and solo travelers looking to understand the island's past.

Proximity: Located in the center of Sant Francesc.

Notes: Entry is usually free, but donations are appreciated.

Can Blai Roman Ruins

The **Can Blai Roman Ruins** offer a glimpse into Formentera's ancient past. This archaeological site features the remains of a Roman fortification, including foundations and walls, believed to have been built between the 2nd and 4th centuries AD. It's one of the few examples of Roman architecture on the island.

What to Do: Walk through the ruins and imagine what life was like during the Roman era. Information boards provide context and historical facts.

Best Time to Visit: Early morning or late afternoon to avoid the heat.

Suitability: Suitable for history lovers and anyone interested in archaeology.

Proximity: Located near the main road between Es Caló and La Mola.

Notes: The site is open-air and free to visit.

Torre de sa Punta Prima Watchtower

The **Torre de sa Punta Prima** is one of several watchtowers built in the 18th century to protect the island from pirate attacks. The tower offers fantastic views of the coastline and is a reminder of Formentera's strategic importance during its history of seafaring and trade.

What to Do: Take in the panoramic views of the coast, and explore the surrounding cliffs for some excellent photo opportunities.

Best Time to Visit: Sunset for a beautiful view over the water.

Chapter 4

Beaches of Formentera

Formentera is known for its stunning coastline, offering some of the most beautiful beaches in Europe. The island's beaches are characterized by white sands and crystal-clear turquoise waters, making them ideal for swimming, sunbathing, and various water sports. Whether you're looking for lively beaches with amenities or hidden coves for a more secluded experience, Formentera has something for everyone. In this chapter, we'll cover the best beaches, hidden coves, and information about the island's relaxed approach to nudity at some beaches.

Best Beaches in Formentera

Playa de Ses Illetes

Playa de Ses Illetes is undoubtedly Formentera's most famous beach and is often listed among the best beaches in Europe. Located on the northern tip of the island within Ses Salines Natural Park, this beach offers soft, white sand and shallow, transparent waters, perfect for swimming, snorkeling, and relaxing.

What to Expect: The beach is part of a protected nature reserve, and its beauty is well-preserved. It stretches out along a narrow strip of land, with the sea visible on both sides, offering stunning views. Ses Illetes is a popular beach, so expect crowds during peak summer months.

Facilities: There are several beach clubs, restaurants, and snack bars nearby, along with sunbeds and parasol rentals.

Suitability: Ideal for families, couples, and solo travelers seeking a top-tier beach experience.

Notes: Parking is available, but there is a small fee to access the beach during the high season as part of the conservation efforts.

Playa de Llevant

Located just a short walk from Ses Illetes, **Playa de Llevant** offers a quieter alternative with the same stunning scenery. Its wide stretch of sand and open space make it perfect for those who prefer a less crowded experience, though the waters can be a bit choppier here compared to Ses Illetes.

What to Expect: Playa de Llevant features similar white sands and turquoise waters, but it is known for being windier, which can result in larger waves. It's a great spot for those who enjoy windsurfing or simply want more space to spread out on the beach.

Facilities: There are a few beach bars nearby, though it's less developed than Ses Illetes. Sunbeds and parasols are available to rent.

Suitability: Great for solo travelers, couples, and windsurfing enthusiasts.

Notes: Due to its location in the nature reserve, it is important to respect the environment and follow local guidelines.

Playa de Migjorn

Playa de Migjorn is one of the longest beaches on the island, stretching along Formentera's southern coast. It offers a more laid-back, less crowded experience compared to the northern beaches. The beach is divided into several smaller coves and sections, making it ideal for visitors looking for variety.

What to Expect: Playa de Migjorn is popular for its diversity of spots, from sandy areas to rocky sections that are great for snorkeling. The calm, shallow waters make it family-friendly, while its vast size ensures you can always find a quiet spot.

Facilities: There are numerous beach bars (chiringuitos), restaurants, and accommodations along the beach, catering to all budgets.

Suitability: Ideal for families, couples, and solo travelers looking for a mix of relaxation and adventure.

Notes: Since it's a long beach, it's easy to find both lively areas and more secluded spots. Parking is readily available.

Cala des Mort

Cala des Mort is a small, picturesque cove tucked away along the coast near Playa de Migjorn. Its name, which means "Cove of Death," refers to the treacherous rocks surrounding the bay, but don't let that deter you—this is one of the most stunning, secluded spots on the island.

What to Expect: The beach is tiny, but its dramatic setting with high cliffs and clear waters makes it a favorite for those seeking a quiet, beautiful spot to escape the crowds. The water is calm, making it great for snorkeling.

Facilities: There are no services here, so be sure to bring your own water and snacks.

Suitability: Perfect for couples and solo travelers looking for a secluded, scenic beach experience.

Notes: Access is via a narrow path, so it's not suitable for those with mobility issues. Arrive early if you want to secure a spot.

Es Caló Beach

Located near the traditional fishing village of Es Caló, **Es Caló Beach** is known for its crystal-clear waters and rocky shoreline, making it one of the best spots for snorkeling on the island. The beach is smaller and more intimate than others, with a rustic charm that draws both locals and tourists.

What to Expect: Es Caló is perfect for those looking to enjoy the underwater world, as the water is exceptionally clear and the marine life is abundant. The beach itself is partly sandy, but there are also rocky sections, providing natural diving platforms into the sea.

Facilities: There are a few restaurants and shops in the nearby village, but no facilities directly on the beach.

Suitability: Great for solo travelers and snorkeling enthusiasts.

Notes: Es Caló can be quite peaceful compared to other beaches, making it ideal for those who want to avoid the summer crowds.

Hidden Coves and Secluded Spots

Formentera's hidden coves and secluded beaches are perfect for travelers seeking peace, privacy, and a chance to immerse themselves in nature. These spots offer a serene alternative to the island's more popular beaches, giving you a chance to experience the beauty of Formentera in a more intimate setting. Whether you're snorkeling in crystal-clear waters, hiking to remote coves, or simply relaxing by the sea, these hidden gems are ideal for those looking to escape the crowds.

Cala en Baster

Cala en Baster is a rocky, secluded cove located near the village of **Sant Ferran**, offering a tranquil retreat for those seeking solitude. The cove's rocky coastline creates dramatic, rugged surroundings, making it more suitable for snorkeling and exploration rather than traditional sunbathing.

What to Expect: The rocky seabed and clear waters make Cala en Baster an excellent snorkeling spot. The cove is home to diverse marine life, and the rocks provide great underwater visibility for spotting fish and other creatures. Although it lacks a sandy beach, the cove's solitude and unspoiled nature attract visitors looking for an off-the-beaten-path experience.

Best For: Adventurers and snorkeling enthusiasts who prefer a quiet, less commercialized spot. Cala en Baster's rocky shoreline offers a unique beauty, and the lack of crowds makes it ideal for a peaceful day by the water.

Accessibility: Cala en Baster is easily reachable by car or bike from Sant Ferran. There are no amenities or services nearby, so it's best to come prepared with water, snacks, and sun protection.

Racó de s'Alga

Located on the uninhabited island of **Espalmador**, just off Formentera's northern coast, **Racó de s'Alga** is a pristine, secluded beach accessible only by boat. The beach is known for its untouched beauty and tranquil atmosphere, making it an idyllic escape for those looking to unwind in a peaceful, remote setting.

What to Expect: The soft, white sands of Racó de s'Alga are framed by shallow, turquoise waters, perfect for swimming and relaxation. As Espalmador is a protected natural reserve, the beach remains undeveloped, ensuring a serene environment free from commercial activity. It's the perfect spot for travelers who want to experience the raw beauty of Formentera's coastline without the typical beach crowds.

Best For: Travelers seeking a secluded beach experience. The calm waters and peaceful atmosphere make Racó de s'Alga an ideal destination for couples, families, and solo travelers looking to disconnect from the outside world.

Accessibility: Racó de s'Alga is accessible by boat from Formentera. You can either join an organized boat tour or rent a private boat. As the island is uninhabited, there are no services, so pack everything you need for the day.

Cala Codolar

Nestled near **La Mola**, **Cala Codolar** is a small, rocky beach that's perfect for adventurous travelers who want to discover one of Formentera's lesser-known spots. This hidden gem boasts clear, calm waters that are ideal for snorkeling, with plenty of marine life to explore.

What to Expect: Cala Codolar's rocky shoreline provides excellent opportunities for snorkeling and exploring the underwater world. The calm waters make it easy to spot fish and other marine creatures, while the surrounding cliffs offer a dramatic backdrop. The beach is small and isolated, so it's rarely crowded, offering plenty of privacy for those looking to escape the busier beaches.

Best For: Adventurers, snorkelers, and those looking for a peaceful retreat away from the main tourist areas. The rocky setting adds to its charm, making it a great spot for photography as well.

Accessibility: Cala Codolar is located near La Mola, and while it's a bit more remote, it's accessible by car or bike. There are no services or facilities, so come prepared with your own supplies.

Cala del Mort

Not to be confused with the nearby Cala des Mort, **Cala del Mort** is a tiny, hidden cove located along Formentera's northern coast. It is accessible via a short hike, which keeps this spot off the radar for most visitors. Its peaceful atmosphere and secluded setting make it a great spot for those looking to unwind in nature.

What to Expect: Cala del Mort is a small, rocky cove that offers a quiet, intimate beach experience. The cove's remote location ensures that it rarely sees many visitors, making it an ideal place for those seeking solitude. While it may not be suitable for swimming due to the rocky terrain, its natural beauty and peaceful surroundings make it worth the visit.

Best For: Solo travelers, couples, or anyone looking to enjoy a private, quiet beach day away from the crowds. The cove's isolated location offers an unparalleled sense of tranquility.

Accessibility: Cala del Mort is accessible only by foot, via a short hike along the northern coast. The hike is relatively easy, but be sure to wear comfortable shoes and bring water, as there are no services at the beach.

Es Ram

Located in one of the more remote parts of Formentera, **Es Ram** is a hidden gem known for its rocky shoreline and stunning turquoise waters. This quiet beach is one of Formentera's best-kept secrets and is perfect for snorkeling and coastal exploration.

What to Expect: Es Ram's rocky coastline is a haven for snorkelers, offering crystal-clear waters and a variety of marine life. The beach itself is peaceful and unspoiled, providing a serene environment for relaxation and nature lovers. While it lacks the soft sands of some of Formentera's more popular beaches, its natural beauty and quiet setting make it a worthwhile destination for those looking to escape the crowds.

Best For: Snorkelers, nature lovers, and anyone seeking a quiet, off-the-beaten-path experience. Es Ram's unspoiled beauty and calm waters make it a great spot for a peaceful day by the sea.

Accessibility: Es Ram is located in a remote area of the island and can be reached by car or bike. The lack of facilities means you'll need to bring your own food, water, and supplies.

Nude Beaches in Formentera: What to Expect

Formentera has long been known for its relaxed attitude toward nudity, and many of the beaches here are unofficially clothing-optional. Nudism is widely accepted on the island, particularly at the more remote and secluded beaches, but it's not mandatory. Here's what to expect if you're visiting a nude beach:

Popular Nude Beaches: Ses Illetes and Playa de Migjorn are two of the most popular beaches where nudism is common. However, it's also practiced on many of the island's more secluded beaches and coves.

Etiquette: If you're visiting a clothing-optional beach, respect others' choices and be discreet with photography. It's also important to understand that nudism is generally more accepted in quieter, less crowded areas, so gauge the vibe of the beach before deciding whether to participate.

Suitability: Nude beaches in Formentera are typically laid-back and inclusive, making them suitable for solo travelers, couples, and even families who are comfortable with the practice.

Chapter 5

Outdoor Activities and Adventures

Formentera's natural beauty makes it the perfect destination for outdoor enthusiasts. Whether you're exploring the island's coastline by boat, hiking its scenic trails, or diving into the crystal-clear waters, there's no shortage of outdoor adventures. This chapter covers the best snorkeling and diving spots, boat excursions, hiking trails, and water sports to ensure that your trip is filled with unforgettable experiences.

Best Snorkeling and Diving Spots

Formentera's clear, turquoise waters and diverse marine life make it one of the best places in the Mediterranean for snorkeling and diving. Whether you're a beginner or an experienced diver, there are several spots around the island where you can explore underwater caves, coral reefs, and abundant sea life.

Es Caló: Known for its rocky coastline and exceptionally clear waters, Es Caló is a favorite among snorkelers. The underwater visibility is excellent, and you'll find plenty of fish, sea urchins, and other marine creatures. The rocky formations also make for interesting underwater landscapes to explore.

Cala Saona: With calm waters and colorful sea life, Cala Saona is a great spot for both snorkeling and diving. The area is home to small reefs and caves, providing plenty of opportunities to see fish and other marine species up close.

Punta Rasa: This area offers deeper waters and more challenging dives. It's ideal for experienced divers looking for underwater rock formations and a chance to see larger species such as groupers and barracudas.

Playa de Migjorn: The long stretch of Playa de Migjorn offers various snorkeling spots with easy access to the water. The seabed here is full of small fish, and the calm, shallow waters make it great for beginners.

Espalmador Island: Accessible by boat, Espalmador's Racó de s'Alga beach offers some of the most unspoiled waters for snorkeling. The area is teeming with marine life and is well-suited for those looking for a secluded experience.

Sailing and Boat Excursions

Sailing around Formentera offers a unique perspective on the island's coastline, with its hidden coves, crystal-clear waters, and remote beaches. Several companies offer boat tours, allowing you to explore areas that are otherwise inaccessible by land.

Catamaran Tours: Sailing in a catamaran around Formentera's coast is one of the most popular excursions. These tours usually stop at secluded beaches and coves, giving you the chance to swim, snorkel, and enjoy the sun. Full-day or half-day options are available, and many include lunch on board.

Sunset Cruises: For a more romantic experience, sunset cruises are available, taking you along the west coast of Formentera to Cala Saona, where you can watch the sun dip below the horizon. These cruises often include drinks and tapas on board.

Boat Excursions to Espalmador: A day trip to Espalmador, a small uninhabited island just north of Formentera, is a popular excursion. The boat ride takes you to this pristine paradise, where you can relax on its white-sand beaches or explore the island's natural mud baths.

Glass-Bottom Boat Tours: For those who want to see Formentera's marine life without diving in, glass-bottom boat tours offer a fantastic way to view the underwater world from above. These tours typically last a couple of hours and include stops at some of the best snorkeling spots.

Day Trips and Island Hopping

Formentera is ideally located for island-hopping adventures, whether it's a day trip to nearby Ibiza or exploring the surrounding islets.

Ibiza: Just a short ferry ride away, Ibiza is perfect for a day trip if you're looking for a change of pace. You can explore Ibiza Town's historic sites, shop in its vibrant markets, or enjoy the island's famous nightlife before heading back to Formentera in the evening.

Espalmador: As mentioned earlier, Espalmador is a popular day trip destination. The island's untouched nature and remote beaches provide a tranquil escape. Many boat tours from Formentera include stops at Espalmador, where you can swim, snorkel, or simply relax on the sand.

Tagomago: Located off the northeastern coast of Ibiza, Tagomago is a private island that's open for exclusive day trips. Although it's not as well-known, it offers luxury boat tours and secluded beach experiences for those looking to splurge on a high-end excursion.

Renting a Boat in Formentera

Renting a boat is a popular way to explore Formentera's hidden coves and remote beaches at your own pace. There are several rental companies on the island that offer a range of boats, from small motorboats to larger yachts, with or without a skipper.

Boat Rentals: Many companies offer small boat rentals that don't require a license, making it easy for tourists to explore the coastline. Prices vary depending on the size of the boat and whether you choose to hire a skipper. A day's rental typically costs between €150 and €500, depending on the type of boat.

Best Routes: Some of the most popular routes include sailing along the north coast to Ses Illetes and Llevant, or heading west towards Cala Saona for stunning sunset views. You can also sail to Espalmador for a day trip.

What to Bring: If you're renting a boat, be sure to bring sun protection, plenty of water, snacks, and snorkeling gear, as many of the coves you'll visit don't have facilities.

Top Hiking and Walking Trails

Formentera's flat landscape and well-marked trails make it an ideal destination for hiking and walking. Whether you're looking for a short scenic walk or a more challenging hike, the island offers several routes with stunning views.

Camí de Sa Pujada: A Historical Path

The **Camí de Sa Pujada** is one of the most famous hiking trails in Formentera, known for its historical significance and stunning views. This ancient path was used for centuries to connect the villages of Es Caló and La Mola, and today it offers a picturesque hiking route.

What to Expect: The trail ascends through a series of stone steps and offers panoramic views of the coastline. Along the way, you'll pass by historical landmarks, including ancient stone walls and the remains of Roman quarries.

Difficulty: Moderate. The hike involves some steep sections, but it's manageable for most hikers.

Best Time to Go: Early morning or late afternoon to avoid the midday heat.

Routes Along the Coastline

For those who prefer coastal walks, Formentera has several routes that follow the shoreline, offering breathtaking views of the sea and access to remote beaches.

Playa de Migjorn to Es Caló: This coastal walk takes you along the southern shore, passing through rocky areas and small coves. It's a relatively easy walk, with plenty of opportunities to stop for a swim along the way.

Ses Illetes to Llevant: This short, easy walk connects two of the island's most famous beaches, offering spectacular views of the sea on both sides. It's perfect for a leisurely stroll and is suitable for all fitness levels.

Cycling Around Formentera

Cycling is one of the most popular ways to explore Formentera, thanks to the island's flat terrain and well-marked bike routes. Many visitors opt to rent a bike for the duration of their stay, allowing them to explore at their own pace.

Bike Rentals and Scenic Routes

Bike Rentals: Renting a bike is affordable and easy, with rental shops available in La Savina, Es Pujols, and other major towns. Prices start from around €10 per day for a standard bike and €20 per day for an electric bike.

Scenic Routes: Formentera has several bike routes that take you through its natural beauty. One of the most popular is the route from La Savina to Ses Illetes, which is an easy ride along a dedicated bike path. Another scenic route is the path from

Sant Francesc Xavier to Cala Saona, offering a mix of coastal views and countryside landscapes.

Windsurfing and Kiteboarding

Formentera's windy conditions, particularly on the northern coast, make it an ideal destination for windsurfing and kiteboarding. Playa de Llevant and the waters around Ses Illetes are particularly popular for these activities, as they offer consistent winds and spacious, open waters.

Windsurfing: Several rental shops around Es Pujols and Llevant Beach offer windsurfing equipment, along with lessons for beginners. Prices start at around €50 for an hour-long lesson, with equipment rental included.

Kiteboarding: While kiteboarding is less common, there are still spots around the island where the conditions are ideal. Playa de Llevant is a favorite among kiteboarders, thanks to its wind conditions and ample space.

Kayaking and Paddleboarding

Kayaking and paddleboarding are fantastic ways to explore Formentera's coastline and its many hidden coves. The calm, clear waters make these activities accessible to beginners, while the island's scenic beauty provides a stunning backdrop for more experienced paddlers.

Kayak Rentals: Kayaks can be rented from several beachside shops, particularly in Es Pujols and Playa de Migjorn. Rates start at around €15 per hour, and many rental shops offer guided tours around the island's coastline.

Paddleboarding: Stand-up paddleboarding (SUP) is a popular activity in Formentera, with rentals available at most major beaches. Playa de Ses Illetes and Cala Saona are

Chapter 6
Formentera for Food Lovers

Formentera's culinary scene is a reflection of its Mediterranean roots, combining fresh, local ingredients with traditional Balearic flavors. Whether you're sampling seafood specialties, indulging in traditional stews, or enjoying a glass of local wine, Formentera offers a rich and varied food experience. This chapter will explore the must-try local dishes, highlight the best places to eat, and introduce you to the island's markets and vineyards.

Must-Try Local Dishes

Formentera's cuisine is heavily influenced by the sea and the island's agricultural traditions. Below are some of the most iconic dishes you should try during your stay.

Peix Sec: Dried Fish

Peix Sec, meaning "dried fish," is one of Formentera's signature dishes. Historically, fishermen would dry their catch under the sun to preserve it. Today, peix sec is a delicacy often served in salads or on its own as a tapa. The fish is typically dried using a traditional process and then rehydrated in olive oil, giving it a rich, intense flavor.

Where to Try It: Many traditional taverns and beachside restaurants serve peix sec as part of a mixed salad or as a standalone dish. Look for it on menus in Es Pujols and Sant Francesc Xavier.

Sofrit Pagès: Traditional Stew

Sofrit Pagès is a hearty traditional stew that originates from the Balearic Islands, including Formentera. This dish is typically made with a mix of meats, such as lamb, chicken, and pork, along with potatoes, garlic, and local spices. It's a flavorful, filling meal that reflects the island's agricultural history.

Where to Try It: You can find Sofrit Pagès in many of Formentera's authentic taverns and family-run restaurants, particularly in Sant Francesc and Es Caló.

Figs and Local Fruits

Formentera's warm climate is ideal for growing figs, and these sweet, juicy fruits are a local favorite. Figs are often eaten fresh, but you'll also find them dried or used in desserts. Other locally grown fruits, such as almonds, apricots, and pomegranates, are also worth trying, either on their own or incorporated into traditional recipes.

Where to Try It: Figs and other local fruits are commonly available at markets and in many dishes served across the island. You'll also find them as part of desserts or snacks in cafes and restaurants.

Seafood Specialties

Given Formentera's location in the Mediterranean, it's no surprise that seafood plays a central role in its cuisine. Local specialties include **calamari a la plancha** (grilled squid), **lobster stew**, and **gambas** (prawns) prepared in various ways.

Fish such as **mero** (grouper) and **besugo** (red bream) are also commonly served grilled or baked.

Where to Try It: Formentera's seafood dishes can be enjoyed at many beachfront eateries and fine dining restaurants, especially those in Es Pujols, La Savina, and Es Caló.

Best Restaurants and Cafes

Whether you're looking for a fine dining experience or a casual beachfront meal, Formentera has a range of dining options to suit all tastes. Here's a look at the best places to eat on the island.

Fine Dining

Formentera has several upscale restaurants where you can enjoy gourmet Mediterranean cuisine with a focus on local ingredients and flavors.

Can Dani: Located near Sant Ferran, Can Dani is one of the most renowned restaurants on the island. It offers a modern take on traditional Formentera dishes, using local ingredients. Expect a fine dining experience with creative presentations and impeccable service.

Beso Beach: Situated at Playa de Cavall d'en Borràs, this upscale beach club and restaurant offers high-end Mediterranean cuisine in a relaxed, stylish setting. It's famous for its seafood dishes and vibrant atmosphere.

Es Molí de Sal: Overlooking the sea near Ses Illetes, this restaurant is known for its spectacular views and excellent seafood. The menu includes local specialties like lobster stew and fresh fish, along with a good selection of wines.

Casual Beachfront Eateries

For a more laid-back dining experience, Formentera's casual beachfront eateries offer delicious food with stunning sea views.

Kiosko 62: Located on Playa de Migjorn, this simple beach shack serves traditional Formentera food in a relaxed setting. Try the grilled squid or the seafood paella while enjoying the beach views.

Lucky Bar: Also on Playa de Migjorn, this casual spot offers a range of Mediterranean dishes, including fresh seafood, salads, and tapas. It's a great place to grab a bite after a swim or a day on the beach.

Juan y Andrea: Situated on Ses Illetes Beach, Juan y Andrea is a popular beachfront restaurant known for its fresh seafood and paella. While pricier than other options, the beachfront location and high-quality food make it worth a visit.

Authentic Local Taverns

For a taste of authentic Formentera cuisine, head to one of the island's traditional taverns. These eateries serve hearty, homemade dishes that reflect the island's agricultural and fishing traditions.

Fonda Pepe: Located in Sant Ferran, Fonda Pepe is a classic tavern that has been a meeting place for locals and travelers for decades. It serves traditional dishes like Sofrit Pagès and grilled meats, alongside local wines.

Ca na Pepa: Situated in Sant Francesc, this cozy tavern offers a menu filled with traditional Formentera dishes made with fresh, local ingredients. It's a great spot to try peix sec and other island specialties.

Local Markets: Fresh Produce and Artisanal Goods

Formentera's local markets are the perfect place to experience the island's vibrant food culture firsthand. You'll find fresh produce, artisanal goods, and locally made products, such as olive oil, honey, and handmade cheeses.

Mercat de Sant Francesc: Located in the capital, this market offers a range of fresh fruits, vegetables, and other local products. It's a great place to pick up fresh figs, almonds, and other Formentera-grown produce.

La Mola Market: Held on Wednesdays and Sundays, this popular market in La Mola features local crafts, artisanal foods, and fresh produce. You can sample and purchase traditional foods, including breads, pastries, and cured meats.

Wine Tasting and Local Vineyards

Formentera is home to several small vineyards that produce excellent wines, thanks to the island's ideal climate for grape growing. The local wine industry is growing, and visitors can enjoy tastings and tours at some of the island's vineyards.

Terramoll Vineyard: Located in La Mola, Terramoll is one of the island's leading wineries. They produce a variety of wines, including whites, reds, and rosés, using locally grown grapes. The vineyard offers guided tours and tastings, allowing you to learn about Formentera's winemaking tradition while enjoying their wines.

Bodegas Cap de Barbaria: Another well-known vineyard, Cap de Barbaria produces high-quality red and rosé wines. The vineyard is set in a picturesque location, and visitors can enjoy wine tastings while overlooking the surrounding countryside.

Vegan and Vegetarian Dining Options

While Formentera's traditional cuisine is largely centered around seafood and meat, the island has seen a growing number of restaurants offering vegan and vegetarian options.

Blat Picat: Located in Sant Ferran, this small cafe serves a variety of vegan and vegetarian dishes, including salads, veggie burgers, and smoothies. It's a great spot for a healthy meal after a day of exploring the island.

S'Eufabi: Situated near Playa de Migjorn, this restaurant offers a mix of traditional Mediterranean and vegetarian dishes. Their menu includes plenty of fresh salads, grilled vegetables, and other plant-based options.

Integral: Located in Es Pujols, Integral offers a range of organic, vegetarian, and vegan options. Their menu includes dishes made with local produce, such as vegetable paella and vegan tapas.

Chapter 7

Shopping in Formentera

Formentera's relaxed atmosphere extends to its shopping scene, where visitors can find a variety of unique items that reflect the island's creative spirit and artisanal traditions. From handcrafted jewelry and pottery to local fashion and beach-inspired decor, Formentera offers a delightful shopping experience. This chapter will guide you through what to buy, where to find local crafts, and the best shopping streets and markets to explore during your visit.

What to Buy: Local Crafts, Fashion, and Souvenirs

Formentera is known for its artisanal craftsmanship and laid-back fashion, making it an ideal destination for picking up unique souvenirs. Below are some of the most popular items to look out for while shopping on the island.

Handmade Jewelry: Local artisans create beautiful pieces using natural materials like shells, stones, and metals. You'll find everything from delicate necklaces to bold, statement pieces that are perfect mementos of your island experience.

Ceramics and Pottery: Formentera has a long tradition of pottery making. Locally made ceramics are popular souvenirs, ranging from decorative plates and bowls to more practical items like mugs and vases. Many of these pieces feature traditional designs inspired by the Mediterranean.

Beachwear and Bohemian Fashion: Formentera's fashion scene is a blend of beach style and bohemian influences. You'll find flowing dresses, tunics, sandals, and wide-brimmed hats that are perfect for a day on the beach. Many local boutiques also sell handmade clothing made from natural fabrics, like linen and cotton.

Handicrafts and Decor: The island is home to many artisans who create unique home decor items, such as handwoven baskets, macramé wall hangings, and driftwood sculptures. These items are perfect for bringing a touch of Formentera's laid-back style to your home.

Organic Cosmetics: Formentera is known for its natural beauty, and several local producers make organic skincare products using ingredients like aloe vera, olive oil, and herbs. These items make great gifts or personal treats to take home.

Artisanal Boutiques: Clothing, Jewelry, and Pottery

Formentera's artisanal boutiques offer a range of handcrafted items, from one-of-a-kind jewelry to locally made pottery. Here are some of the best boutiques to visit during your shopping trip.

Majoral: Located in Sant Francesc, Majoral is a well-known jewelry boutique that specializes in handcrafted pieces inspired by the natural beauty of Formentera. Their designs often incorporate organic shapes and materials, making each piece unique.

Atelier de Formentera: This boutique in Es Pujols offers a range of fashion and accessories with a focus on sustainability. You'll find handmade clothing, bags, and jewelry crafted from natural materials.

Cerámica de Formentera: If you're looking for locally made ceramics, this small pottery studio in Sant Ferran offers a variety of beautiful, handcrafted items. Their designs are inspired by the island's colors and textures, and you can purchase anything from decorative tiles to functional pottery.

Casa Tapas: Located in Sant Francesc, this boutique is known for its selection of bohemian-style clothing and home decor. It's a great spot to pick up a flowing beach dress or a handmade basket to take home.

Estrella: Another boutique in Es Pujols, Estrella offers a mix of locally made jewelry, clothing, and accessories. Their collection is known for its laid-back, beachy vibe, perfect for capturing the essence of Formentera's style.

Beach Markets: Handicrafts and Unique Finds

Formentera's beach markets are a must-visit for travelers looking for unique, handmade items and a more casual shopping experience. These markets are often held along the island's main beaches or in small villages, where local artisans sell their crafts.

La Mola Artisan Market: Held every Wednesday and Sunday from May to October, the La Mola Artisan Market is one of the most popular shopping destinations on the island. Located in the village of El Pilar de la Mola, this market offers a wide variety of handcrafted goods, including jewelry, ceramics, leather items, and textiles. Many of the items are made by local artisans, ensuring that you're purchasing something authentic and unique to Formentera.

Es Pujols Beach Market: Located along the promenade in Es Pujols, this market is known for its mix of beachwear, handmade jewelry, and souvenirs. It's a great place to browse after spending the day at the beach, with plenty of vendors offering handcrafted items that make perfect gifts or keepsakes.

Sant Ferran Night Market: This smaller market, held in the evenings during the summer months, offers a variety of handicrafts, including paintings, jewelry, and home decor items. It's a quieter alternative to the La Mola market, but still offers a range of unique items created by local artisans.

Playa de Migjorn Market: This market is a bit more laid-back and is perfect for those looking for handmade crafts, beachwear, and art. It's a great spot to pick up some unique items while enjoying the relaxed beach atmosphere.

Shopping Streets and Markets in Es Pujols and Sant Francesc

Formentera's two main shopping hubs are Es Pujols and Sant Francesc, where you'll find a mix of boutiques, markets, and local shops.

Es Pujols: As one of the busiest towns on the island, Es Pujols is home to a variety of boutiques and markets. Along the beachfront promenade, you'll find shops selling beachwear, jewelry, and souvenirs, as well as several beach markets that operate in the evening. The town has a vibrant, lively atmosphere, making it a fun place to explore after a day at the beach.

Sant Francesc Xavier: For a more relaxed shopping experience, head to Sant Francesc, the island's capital. The narrow streets are lined with boutiques and shops offering local crafts, clothing, and home decor. The town square is home to the Mercat de Sant Francesc, where you can find fresh produce, handmade goods, and artisanal items. Sant Francesc is also a great place to pick up unique gifts and souvenirs while enjoying a leisurely stroll through the town.

Chapter 7

Shopping in Formentera

Formentera offers more than just stunning beaches and natural beauty—it's also a haven for shoppers looking for unique, handcrafted items that reflect the island's laid-back vibe and artistic spirit. Whether you're hunting for local crafts, stylish beachwear, or handmade jewelry, Formentera's markets and boutiques have something for everyone. This chapter focuses on what to buy, where to shop, and the best markets to explore during your visit.

What to Buy: Local Crafts, Fashion, and Souvenirs

When shopping in Formentera, you'll find a wide range of artisanal products that are perfect for souvenirs or gifts. Here's a look at the most popular items to bring back from the island:

Handmade Jewelry: Local artisans create stunning pieces using natural materials such as shells, stones, and metals. These unique designs often reflect the island's natural beauty, making them perfect mementos.

Bohemian Beachwear: Formentera's fashion is a blend of beach style and bohemian influences. You'll find flowing dresses, tunics, sandals, and wide-brimmed hats made from natural fabrics like cotton and linen, perfect for the warm Mediterranean climate.

Local Ceramics: Formentera is home to several talented potters who create beautiful handmade ceramics. These include decorative plates, bowls, and mugs featuring traditional Mediterranean patterns and colors.

Home Decor: You'll also find handcrafted home decor items, such as woven baskets, macramé wall hangings, and driftwood sculptures, all of which reflect Formentera's relaxed and rustic charm.

Organic Skincare: Many local producers on the island make organic cosmetics and skincare products, often using aloe vera, olive oil, and herbs grown locally. These products make for great gifts or a personal treat.

Artisanal Boutiques: Clothing, Jewelry, and Pottery

Formentera is known for its independent boutiques, where you can find a wide range of locally crafted items, including jewelry, clothing, and pottery. These boutiques offer a more personalized shopping experience, with many items made by hand on the island.

Majoral: Located in Sant Francesc, Majoral is a boutique specializing in handcrafted jewelry inspired by Formentera's natural landscape. Their unique pieces are made from high-quality materials and make for a special keepsake.

Atelier 44: This boutique in Es Pujols offers a selection of handmade jewelry, clothing, and accessories. Many of the items are made using sustainable materials, and the shop emphasizes local craftsmanship.

Cerámica Artesanal de Formentera: This pottery studio, located in Sant Ferran, offers beautiful handcrafted ceramics. Their designs often feature the island's iconic colors and shapes, making them a perfect addition to your home.

Sés Roques: Located in Es Pujols, this boutique offers a variety of clothing and accessories, with a focus on bohemian and beach-inspired styles. You'll find flowing dresses, sandals, and handmade jewelry, ideal for the island's relaxed lifestyle.

Estrella de Formentera: This boutique specializes in handmade items such as jewelry and clothing. Their collections often feature organic fabrics and materials sourced locally, making them a great choice for eco-conscious shoppers.

Beach Markets: Handicrafts and Unique Finds

For a more relaxed shopping experience, Formentera's beach markets are a must-visit. These markets feature a variety of handmade goods, from jewelry to clothing, and offer an authentic glimpse into the island's artisanal culture.

La Mola Artisan Market: Held every Wednesday and Sunday from May to October, the La Mola market is one of the most popular artisan markets on the island. Here, you'll find a wide range of handcrafted goods, including pottery, jewelry, clothing, and leather items. Many of the items are made by local artisans, ensuring that your purchase is one-of-a-kind.

Es Pujols Beach Market: Located along the promenade in Es Pujols, this market offers a mix of beachwear, jewelry, and souvenirs. It's a great place to browse in the late afternoon or evening, with many local artisans selling their creations.

Sant Ferran Night Market: This smaller, more intimate market is held in the evenings during the summer months. It offers a range of handicrafts, including art, jewelry, and home decor. It's a quieter alternative to the La Mola market, but still offers a variety of unique finds.

Playa de Migjorn Market: A more laid-back market located near Playa de Migjorn, this is the perfect spot to find handcrafted beachwear, jewelry, and art. It's a great way to pick up some unique items while enjoying a day by the sea.

Shopping Streets and Markets in Es Pujols and Sant Francesc

The main shopping hubs in Formentera are **Es Pujols** and **Sant Francesc Xavier**, where you'll find a variety of boutiques, markets, and local shops offering everything from beachwear to artisanal crafts.

Es Pujols: As the island's busiest resort town, Es Pujols is home to a variety of shops and markets. The beachfront promenade is lined with boutiques selling beachwear, jewelry, and souvenirs, as well as several evening markets that are perfect for browsing after a day at the beach. The lively atmosphere makes it a fun place to shop and people-watch.

Sant Francesc Xavier: For a more laid-back shopping experience, head to Sant Francesc, the island's capital. The narrow streets are home to charming boutiques offering local crafts, bohemian clothing, and home decor. The town square hosts the **Mercat de Sant Francesc**, a small market where you can find fresh produce, handmade goods, and artisanal items. Sant Francesc is the perfect place for a leisurely shopping trip, with plenty of cafes where you can relax after a day of browsing.

Chapter 8

Cultural Experiences and Events

Formentera may be a small island, but it has a rich cultural heritage that can be experienced through its local festivals, traditional music and dance, and thriving art scene. This chapter explores the island's most important cultural events, art galleries, and unique experiences that will give visitors a deeper understanding of Formentera's traditions and contemporary cultural landscape.

Local Festivals and Celebrations

Formentera hosts several vibrant festivals throughout the year, each offering a unique insight into the island's traditions and way of life. These celebrations often include music, dance, food, and religious processions, providing an opportunity for visitors to experience the island's culture firsthand.

Festa de Sant Jaume (July)

The **Festa de Sant Jaume** is one of Formentera's most important annual celebrations, held in honor of the island's patron saint, St. James. Taking place every July in the capital, Sant Francesc Xavier, this festival is a lively event that brings together locals and tourists for a week of festivities.

What to Expect: The festival includes religious processions, live music performances, traditional dances, and fireworks.

Street parties and outdoor concerts fill the town square, and local restaurants often serve special menus during the event.

Best For: Visitors interested in experiencing local traditions, music, and food. The festival's vibrant atmosphere makes it enjoyable for all ages.

Festa de Sant Ferran (May)

The **Festa de Sant Ferran**, celebrated in May, honors the town of Sant Ferran and its patron saint. It's a smaller, more intimate festival than Sant Jaume, but it's no less festive. The event is centered around the town's church and plaza, where locals gather for celebrations that reflect the island's traditions.

What to Expect: The festival includes religious ceremonies, traditional music and folk dancing, and lively street fairs with local food and artisan stalls. There are also activities for children, making it a family-friendly event.

Best For: Visitors looking for a more local experience, as this festival tends to attract fewer tourists than Festa de Sant Jaume.

Traditional Music and Dance Performances

Traditional Balearic music and dance play an important role in Formentera's cultural identity. Throughout the year, visitors can enjoy live performances of **Ball Pagès**, a traditional dance that dates back centuries, and **xeremies**, a form of traditional bagpipe music unique to the Balearic Islands.

Ball Pagès: This folk dance is performed in traditional costume, with women wearing long skirts and ornate jewelry, and men in simple white shirts and black trousers. The dance is characterized by its slow, graceful movements, accompanied by live traditional music.

Where to See Performances: Traditional music and dance performances are often held during local festivals and cultural events. In the summer months, you may also find regular performances in Sant Francesc or Es Pujols, where you can witness Ball Pagès and other forms of folk music.

Art Galleries and Cultural Centers

Formentera has long been a haven for artists and creatives, and the island's art scene reflects this. There are several art galleries and cultural centers where visitors can explore contemporary art, traditional crafts, and rotating exhibitions by local and international artists.

Contemporary Art Scene

Formentera's contemporary art scene is thriving, with many galleries showcasing the work of both local and international artists. The island's natural beauty has long inspired painters, sculptors, and photographers, and this is reflected in the diverse range of art available to view and purchase.

La Mola Art Gallery: Located in El Pilar de la Mola, this small gallery showcases a mix of contemporary art, including paintings, sculptures, and photography. Many of the works on display are inspired by Formentera's landscapes and seascapes.

Galería Blanca: Situated in Sant Francesc, Galería Blanca features contemporary art from local artists. The gallery often hosts exhibitions and events, making it a vibrant part of the island's art scene.

Open-Air Exhibitions

Formentera's warm climate and natural beauty make it an ideal setting for open-air art exhibitions. These exhibitions often feature sculptures and installations placed in outdoor locations, allowing visitors to enjoy both art and nature simultaneously.

Es Pujols Promenade: In the summer months, Es Pujols hosts open-air art exhibitions along the promenade, featuring sculptures and installations by local artists. This casual setting allows visitors to explore the artwork at their own pace while enjoying the coastal scenery.

Cultural Walks in Sant Francesc: Occasionally, the streets of Sant Francesc become an open-air gallery, with artists displaying their works in the town's squares and public spaces. These cultural walks are usually part of larger festivals or events.

Guided Cultural Tours

Formentera's rich history and culture can be further explored through guided tours, which offer in-depth insights into the island's heritage. These tours are led by local experts and cover various aspects of Formentera's culture, from its historical landmarks to its artistic traditions.

Historical Tours of Sant Francesc: Explore Formentera's capital with a knowledgeable guide who can take you through the town's historical sites, including the Església de Sant Francesc Xavier, and explain the island's religious and cultural heritage.

Art and Culture Walks: Some guided tours focus on the island's art scene, taking visitors to key galleries and studios where they can meet local artists and learn about the creative process.

Cultural and Nature Tours: For those interested in both Formentera's culture and natural environment, combined tours are available that explore both the island's cultural landmarks and its stunning landscapes. These tours often include visits to historical sites, such as La Mola Lighthouse, as well as natural wonders like the Ses Salines Natural Park.

Chapter 9

Nightlife and Entertainment

Formentera's nightlife may not be as famous as its neighboring island Ibiza, but it offers a unique, laid-back atmosphere that makes it perfect for those seeking a more relaxed and intimate evening experience. From beach clubs to live music venues, Formentera's nightlife scene provides a blend of sophistication and casual charm. This chapter will guide you through the best places to enjoy an evening out, from beachside bars to special events like full moon parties and local festivals.

Best Beach Clubs and Lounges

Formentera's beach clubs and lounges offer a stylish way to enjoy the island's beautiful sunsets and balmy nights. These venues provide the perfect mix of great music, refreshing cocktails, and a vibrant atmosphere, often right on the beach.

Beso Beach: Located on Playa de Cavall d'en Borràs, Beso Beach is one of the island's most popular beach clubs. Known for its lively atmosphere and stunning location, this spot offers great food, drinks, and music. As the sun sets, the party picks up, with DJs spinning Balearic beats well into the night. Beso Beach attracts a trendy crowd, making it perfect for those looking for a fashionable but relaxed evening out.

Blue Bar: Set on Playa de Migjorn, Blue Bar is a legendary spot on Formentera's nightlife circuit. The beach bar transitions from a daytime lounge to a lively venue at night, offering excellent cocktails and a mix of live music and DJ sets. With a backdrop of glowing blue lights and a scenic beach view, Blue Bar creates a unique ambiance that's perfect for a casual night of dancing and socializing.

10.7 Beach Club: Also located on Playa de Migjorn, 10.7 Beach Club is a stylish beachside venue offering a relaxed vibe during the day and a lively atmosphere at night. It's a great spot to sip cocktails, enjoy Mediterranean cuisine, and watch the sunset. As the evening progresses, the beach club comes alive with music, making it a go-to spot for a night out.

Chezz Gerdi: Situated in Es Pujols, Chezz Gerdi offers a chic setting with a beautiful waterfront view. Known for its gourmet cuisine and top-notch cocktails, this lounge is a great place to start the night. After dinner, the bar area becomes a lively spot for drinks and music, often featuring live DJs. Its stylish decor and relaxed vibe make it a favorite for those looking for an upscale yet laid-back night out.

Pirata Beach Club: Located near Es Pujols, Pirata Beach Club offers a more relaxed, bohemian vibe. With its rustic beach setting, hammocks, and cozy seating areas, it's a great spot to unwind after a day at the beach. The club often hosts live music and DJ nights, making it a fun yet low-key option for a night out.

Live Music Venues

Formentera has a vibrant live music scene, with many bars and venues hosting performances from local and international musicians. Whether you're into acoustic sets, jazz, or Balearic beats, there's a venue for every taste.

Fonda Pepe: This iconic venue in Sant Ferran has long been a hub for live music on the island. Known for its bohemian atmosphere, Fonda Pepe attracts a diverse crowd of locals and visitors alike. The venue hosts regular live music nights, featuring everything from acoustic guitar performances to full bands. It's a great place to experience the island's laid-back, artistic vibe while enjoying a drink or two.

Sa Panxa: Located in Sant Ferran, Sa Panxa is a popular spot for live music and offers a wide variety of genres, from jazz to rock. The intimate setting makes it a great place to relax and enjoy a drink while listening to live performances. Check the schedule in advance, as the venue frequently features both local musicians and visiting artists.

Es Pujols Beach Bars: Many of the beach bars in Es Pujols host live music during the summer months, particularly in the evenings. Venues like Blanco and Chezz Gerdi often feature live acoustic sets or DJ performances, making them great spots to enjoy a relaxed night of music by the sea.

Bars with a View: Formentera's Rooftop Bars

For those who enjoy breathtaking views while sipping a cocktail, Formentera's rooftop bars provide the perfect setting to unwind and watch the sunset.

Kiosko Pirata Rooftop: Situated in Es Pujols, Kiosko Pirata offers one of the best rooftop views on the island. With a relaxed atmosphere and great cocktails, it's the perfect place to enjoy a sunset drink while overlooking the beach. The rooftop bar is known for its casual vibe, making it ideal for solo travelers or couples looking for a peaceful evening.

Blanco Rooftop Bar: Located in Es Pujols, Blanco is a chic rooftop bar offering stunning views over the coastline. It's a great spot to enjoy a glass of wine or a signature cocktail while taking in the sunset. The bar often hosts live DJs, creating a lively yet relaxed atmosphere as the evening progresses.

Hotel Cala Saona Rooftop: For a more luxurious experience, head to the rooftop bar at Hotel Cala Saona. This upscale venue offers panoramic views of Cala Saona Beach, making it a perfect spot for a romantic evening. The rooftop features a well-curated cocktail menu, and the setting is ideal for a relaxing night out with a view.

Casual Beachfront Bars and Cocktail Spots

Formentera's beachfront bars are ideal for those seeking a laid-back atmosphere with good drinks and great views. These casual spots offer a perfect end to a day spent lounging on the beach.

Kiosko 62: Located on Playa de Migjorn, Kiosko 62 is a beloved beach bar offering casual vibes, cold drinks, and stunning views. It's a simple, no-frills spot where you can grab a beer or a mojito and relax with your feet in the sand as the sun sets over the horizon.

Lucky Bar: Also situated on Playa de Migjorn, Lucky Bar offers a range of cocktails and light snacks in a relaxed beachfront setting. It's a popular spot for those looking to wind down after a long day of swimming and sunbathing. The bar's laid-back atmosphere makes it a great place to enjoy a quiet evening with friends.

La Fragata Beach Bar: Located near Es Pujols, this casual beachfront bar offers delicious cocktails and a great view of the sea. The bar is known for its relaxed vibe, and it's a favorite spot for both locals and tourists to enjoy drinks and snacks by the water.

Sa Sequi Beach Bar: This small, rustic beach bar near La Savina is perfect for those looking for a low-key evening by the sea. The bar serves simple but delicious food and drinks, and the setting is peaceful and intimate.

Special Events: Full Moon Parties and Festivals

Formentera's nightlife also includes special events and festivals, many of which take advantage of the island's beautiful natural surroundings. One of the most popular events on the island is the **Full Moon Party**, a beach celebration held on select nights throughout the summer.

Full Moon Parties: These events typically take place on Playa de Migjorn or Es Pujols, where beach clubs and bars host lively parties under the full moon. The parties often feature live DJs, bonfires, and dancing on the beach. While not as wild as Ibiza's legendary parties, Formentera's full moon events offer a fun and more relaxed alternative.

Local Festivals: In addition to the full moon parties, Formentera hosts several local festivals throughout the year, many of which include evening events and celebrations. The **Festa de Sant Jaume** in July is one of the island's biggest festivals and features live music, street parties, and fireworks. These festivals offer a great opportunity to experience Formentera's nightlife in a more cultural setting.

Chapter 10

Day Trips and Excursions from Formentera

While Formentera is a small island, its location makes it an ideal starting point for various day trips and excursions to nearby destinations. Whether you're interested in exploring the vibrant island of Ibiza, sailing to the uninhabited island of Espalmador, or discovering hidden islets and coves, Formentera's proximity to these places ensures you can experience more of the Balearic Islands' beauty. In this chapter, we'll cover how to plan your day trips, including ferry connections, sailing excursions, and hidden gems waiting to be explored.

Exploring Ibiza: How to Plan a Day Trip

Formentera's close proximity to Ibiza makes it easy to plan a day trip to its lively neighbor. While Ibiza is famous for its nightlife, it also offers plenty of cultural attractions, beautiful beaches, and historic landmarks worth exploring during the day.

Getting There: Regular ferries operate between Formentera and Ibiza, with the journey taking about 30 minutes. Ferries depart from La Savina port in Formentera and arrive at Ibiza Town (Eivissa). Tickets can be booked in advance or on the day of travel, but during peak summer months, it's advisable to book early.

What to Do in Ibiza: Start your day by exploring the UNESCO World Heritage site **Dalt Vila**, the old town of Ibiza. The narrow, cobbled streets and historic buildings offer a glimpse into Ibiza's rich history. Afterward, you can head to the island's famous beaches, such as **Talamanca Beach**, located close to Ibiza Town. For those interested in shopping, the **Las Dalias Hippy Market** in Sant Carles is worth a visit, offering handmade crafts, jewelry, and clothing. You can also visit the quieter villages like **Santa Gertrudis** for a more relaxed, local experience.

Best Time to Visit: A day trip to Ibiza is best planned during the week to avoid the weekend crowds, especially in the summer. Most attractions and beaches can be enjoyed during daylight hours, making it easy to return to Formentera by the evening.

Sailing to Espalmador Island

Espalmador Island is a small, uninhabited islet just off the northern coast of Formentera. Known for its pristine beaches and natural beauty, it's a popular day-trip destination for visitors seeking tranquility and untouched nature.

Getting There: Espalmador is accessible by boat, and several boat tours operate daily from Formentera. Alternatively, you can rent your own boat or charter a private yacht for the day. The trip from La Savina to Espalmador takes about 20 minutes, and once you arrive, you'll be greeted by white sand beaches and crystal-clear waters.

What to Do on Espalmador: The island is famous for its **Racó de s'Alga Beach**, where you can swim, snorkel, or simply relax on the soft sands. The waters are shallow and calm, making it perfect for families and those looking for a peaceful beach experience. Espalmador is also known for its **mud baths**, where visitors can cover themselves in natural clay mud before rinsing off in the sea. While the island is uninhabited and lacks facilities, its natural beauty makes it an unforgettable day trip destination.

Tips for Visiting: Since there are no restaurants or shops on the island, make sure to bring your own food, water, and sun protection. Respect the island's environment and take any litter with you when you leave, as Espalmador is part of a protected natural reserve.

Ferry Connections to Mainland Spain

While Formentera is primarily connected to Ibiza, it's also possible to take a ferry from Ibiza to mainland Spain, making a day trip or overnight excursion to cities like **Denia**, **Valencia**, or **Barcelona** a viable option.

Denia: Denia is the closest point on the mainland to Formentera, and ferries run regularly between Ibiza and Denia. The journey takes around 2.5 hours. Once in Denia, you can explore its historic castle, beautiful beaches, and charming old town. Denia is also known for its excellent seafood restaurants.

Valencia: A longer ferry ride of approximately 5 hours takes you to Valencia, one of Spain's largest cities. Known for its futuristic architecture, historic old town, and beautiful beaches, Valencia is a vibrant destination with plenty to offer for a day or weekend trip.

Barcelona: For those willing to travel overnight, ferries also connect Ibiza to Barcelona. The journey takes around 8 hours, making it more suitable for an overnight or multi-day trip. Barcelona is famous for its architectural landmarks, including **La Sagrada Familia**, **Park Güell**, and **La Rambla**, making it an ideal city to explore if you have more time.

Discovering Nearby Islets and Hidden Coves

Formentera is surrounded by several small islets and hidden coves that are perfect for a day of exploration by boat. Renting a boat or joining an organized tour allows you to discover these secluded spots, many of which are inaccessible by land.

S'Espalmador and Ses Illetes: While Espalmador is the most well-known of Formentera's surrounding islets, the area around **Ses Illetes Beach** also offers smaller coves and islets worth exploring. Sailing around this area gives you access to remote beaches and coves where you can swim, snorkel, or simply relax in the serene surroundings.

Es Vedrà: A small rocky island off the coast of Ibiza, **Es Vedrà** is famous for its striking beauty and mystique. Many boat tours from Formentera include a visit to Es Vedrà, where you can view the island's rugged cliffs and hear about the myths and legends associated with the area.

Cala Saona's Hidden Coves: The western coast of Formentera is home to several hidden coves that can be reached by boat from **Cala Saona**. These quiet spots are perfect for a more private beach experience, away from the crowds of the main beaches.

Punta Rasa and Punta Prima: For those who enjoy snorkeling and diving, the waters around **Punta Rasa** and **Punta Prima** are teeming with marine life. These areas are best explored by boat, and you'll find several coves and underwater caves to explore during the day.

Chapter 11

Practical Information and Traveler Tips

To make the most of your trip to Formentera, it's important to be well-prepared with practical information on how to get around, communicate with locals, and manage your travel essentials. This chapter covers key details, from transportation options to staying connected and understanding the local language, ensuring your visit is as smooth and enjoyable as possible.

Getting Around Formentera

Formentera is a small island, and getting around is relatively easy. The island's flat terrain and compact size make it perfect for exploring by scooter, car, bicycle, or on foot. There are several transportation options to choose from, depending on your preferences and the type of experience you're seeking.

Renting Scooters and Cars

Renting a scooter or car is one of the most convenient ways to explore Formentera, giving you the freedom to visit remote beaches and hidden coves at your own pace. Scooters are especially popular, as they are affordable and perfect for navigating the island's narrow roads.

Scooter Rentals: Scooters can be rented at various locations around the island, including La Savina (the port), Es Pujols, and Sant Francesc. Prices start at around €20 to €30 per day, with discounts available for longer rentals. Scooters are ideal for solo travelers or couples looking for an affordable and easy way to get around.

Car Rentals: For families or groups, renting a car might be more convenient. Car rentals are available from several companies at La Savina and other major towns. Prices vary depending on the type of vehicle and rental duration, but expect to pay between €40 and €70 per day. Keep in mind that parking can be limited in some areas, especially during peak season.

Driving Tips: Formentera's roads are generally in good condition, but be cautious when driving on narrow or winding routes. The island's relaxed pace extends to its roads, so be mindful of cyclists and pedestrians, especially in more populated areas.

Public Transport Options

Formentera has a limited public transport network, but buses are available for those who prefer not to drive. The island's bus service connects key towns and beaches, making it a viable option for budget-conscious travelers.

Bus Routes: The main bus routes connect La Savina, Es Pujols, Sant Francesc, and several of the island's beaches, including Playa de Migjorn and Ses Illetes. Buses run frequently during the summer months but may be less frequent in the off-season.

Ticket Prices: A single bus journey costs around €1.80 to €2.50, depending on the route. Day passes are also available for unlimited travel, making them a convenient option for those planning to use the bus multiple times in one day.

Biking and Walking Routes

Formentera's flat terrain and well-marked cycling paths make it ideal for exploring by bike or on foot. Many visitors choose to rent bicycles to get around, enjoying the island's natural beauty at a slower pace.

Bike Rentals: Bicycles can be rented at various locations, with prices starting at around €10 to €15 per day. Electric bikes are also available for those who prefer a more effortless ride.

Scenic Routes: Formentera has several designated cycling and walking routes that take you through the island's most scenic areas. Popular routes include the path from La Savina to Ses Illetes Beach and the coastal route along Playa de Migjorn.

Walking Trails: Formentera is home to several walking trails, including the historical **Camí de Sa Pujada**, which offers stunning views of the coastline. These trails are well-marked, making them suitable for hikers of all experience levels.

Essential Travel Apps for Formentera

Travel apps can make navigating Formentera easier and more enjoyable. Here are some recommended apps that will help you during your trip:

Google Maps: A must-have for navigation, Google Maps provides up-to-date information on routes, walking paths, and public transport schedules. It's particularly helpful for finding remote beaches and hidden spots.

Formentera Bus: This app provides real-time information on bus schedules and routes across the island. It's particularly useful if you plan to rely on public transport.

Tripadvisor: For restaurant recommendations, activity ideas, and traveler reviews, Tripadvisor is a great resource. Use it to find the best places to eat and explore based on other travelers' experiences.

XE Currency Converter: For currency conversion, XE Currency is a handy app that helps you quickly convert prices from euros to your home currency.

Google Translate: Although many locals speak English, having Google Translate on hand can help with basic communication, especially if you want to practice Spanish or Catalan.

Language Tips: Basic Spanish and Catalan Phrases

The official languages of Formentera are **Spanish** and **Catalan**, and many locals speak both. While English is widely understood in tourist areas, learning a few basic phrases in

Spanish and Catalan can enhance your experience and help you connect with locals.

Here are some useful phrases:

Hola (Spanish) / **Bon dia** (Catalan): Hello / Good morning

Gracias (Spanish) / **Gràcies** (Catalan): Thank you

Por favor (Spanish) / **Si us plau** (Catalan): Please

¿Dónde está la playa? (Spanish) / **On és la platja?** (Catalan): Where is the beach?

¿Cuánto cuesta? (Spanish) / **Quant costa?** (Catalan): How much does it cost?

Even if you just use these simple greetings and polite expressions, locals will appreciate the effort.

Currency Exchange and Banking

Formentera uses the **euro (€)** as its currency, and most businesses accept credit and debit cards. However, it's always a good idea to carry some cash, particularly in more remote areas where card payments may not be accepted.

ATMs: ATMs are available in major towns such as La Savina, Es Pujols, and Sant Francesc. Make sure to withdraw cash when you're in these areas, as ATMs can be scarce in more rural locations.

Currency Exchange: Currency exchange services are available at La Savina port and in some banks. However, it's often more convenient and cost-effective to use an ATM to withdraw euros directly.

Tipping: Tipping is not obligatory in Spain, but it's appreciated. A tip of 5% to 10% is common in restaurants and for taxi drivers.

Staying Connected: SIM Cards and Wi-Fi Access

Staying connected during your stay in Formentera is easy, as the island has good mobile coverage and plenty of Wi-Fi hotspots.

SIM Cards: If you plan to stay for an extended period or need consistent access to mobile data, purchasing a local SIM card is recommended. SIM cards can be bought at phone shops in La Savina or Sant Francesc, with several providers offering prepaid plans.

Wi-Fi: Many hotels, cafes, and restaurants offer free Wi-Fi, making it easy to stay connected without a SIM card. However, if you're planning to visit remote areas or beaches, mobile data may be necessary, as Wi-Fi can be limited in those regions.

Final Travel Checklist

Before heading to Formentera, make sure you've packed and prepared all the essentials for a stress-free trip:

Travel Documents: Ensure you have your passport, travel insurance, and any required visas. Keep digital copies of important documents, including flight tickets and accommodation details.

Cash and Cards: Bring some euros in cash for small purchases and rural areas. Ensure your debit and credit cards work in Europe, and notify your bank of your travel plans to avoid any issues.

Sunscreen and Sun Protection: Formentera's sunny weather calls for high-SPF sunscreen, a hat, and sunglasses to protect against the strong Mediterranean sun.

Comfortable Shoes: Whether you plan to explore the island by bike, on foot, or by scooter, comfortable shoes are essential for a full day of activities.

Reusable Water Bottle: Staying hydrated is important, especially if you're spending time on the beach or hiking. A reusable water bottle is also an eco-friendly option.

Travel Apps: Download all the essential travel apps mentioned earlier to make navigating and planning your trip easier.

Conclusion

Embracing the Laid-Back Island Life

Formentera is a destination that invites you to slow down and immerse yourself in its natural beauty, vibrant culture, and relaxed atmosphere. The island's pristine beaches, clear waters, and scenic landscapes offer the perfect backdrop for a peaceful getaway. Whether you're lounging on the white sands of Ses Illetes, exploring hidden coves by boat, or enjoying a meal at a beachfront restaurant, the island's charm lies in its simplicity and unspoiled environment.

Formentera's rich culture, local festivals, and welcoming community make it more than just a beach destination. By experiencing the island's traditional music, art, and food, you'll gain a deeper connection to its history and way of life. The island's sustainable tourism efforts also ensure that future generations will be able to enjoy its beauty, making it an ideal destination for eco-conscious travelers.

Final Tips for a Memorable Journey to Formentera

Plan Ahead for Peak Season: If you're visiting during the summer months, be sure to book your accommodation, transportation, and restaurants in advance to avoid disappointment, as the island can get busy.

Embrace Local Traditions: Take part in local festivals, try traditional dishes like peix sec, and support local artisans by purchasing handmade crafts. Engaging with the island's culture will make your trip even more memorable.

Pack for Comfort: Bring light, breathable clothing, sunscreen, and comfortable shoes for exploring. A reusable water bottle and eco-friendly toiletries will also help reduce your environmental impact.

Explore Beyond the Beaches: While Formentera is famous for its beaches, don't miss out on its hiking trails, cultural tours, and local markets. Exploring the island's interior will give you a more rounded experience.

Respect the Island's Environment: Formentera's natural beauty is part of what makes it special. Respect protected areas, minimize waste, and consider eco-friendly transport options like biking or walking to reduce your impact.

Printed in Great Britain
by Amazon

60690443R00060